W9-BIA-771

Australia

by Rebecca Hirsch

Content Consultant
Associate Professor Baden Offord, Ph.D.
Southern Cross University

Reading Consultant
Jeanne Clidas
Reading Specialist

Children's Press®
An Imprint of Scholastic Inc.
New York • Toronto • London • Auckland • Sydney • Mexico City
New Delhi • Hong Kong • Danbury, Connecticut

Library of Congress Cataloging-in-Publication Data
Hirsch, Rebecca E.
  Australia / by Rebecca Hirsch.
     p. cm. – (Rookie read-about geography)
  Includes index.
  ISBN 978-0-531-28978-5 (lib.bdg.) – ISBN 978-0-531-29278-5
(pbk.)
  1. Australia–Juvenile literature. 2. Australia–Geography–Juvenile
literature. I. Title.

  DU96.H56 2012
  919.4–dc23

                          2012013401

Photographs © 2013: age fotostock: 30 (Hans Reinhard/Lithium), 10
(LEMAIRE Stphane/hem), 4 (Sylvain Grandadam); Alamy Images/Hollis
Photography.com: 12; Corbis Images/Robert Essel NYC: cover main;
Dreamstime/Celso Diniz: cover kangaroo; Getty Images/Harvey Lloyd/
Taxi: 29; OceanwideImages.com/Gary Bell: 24; Shutterstock, Inc.: 16, 31
top right (covenant), 8 (Jan Kratochvila), 26, 31 bottom right (Johan
Larson), 18, 31 bottom left (Ralph Loesche); Superstock, Inc.: 22 (Ignacio
Palacios/age fotostock), 14, 31 top left (Robert Harding Picture Library),
20 (Steve Vidler).

Map by Matt Kania/www.maphero.com

Table of Contents

People hike in Uluru National Park.

Welcome to Australia!

Australia is the world's smallest continent. It is both a continent and a country.

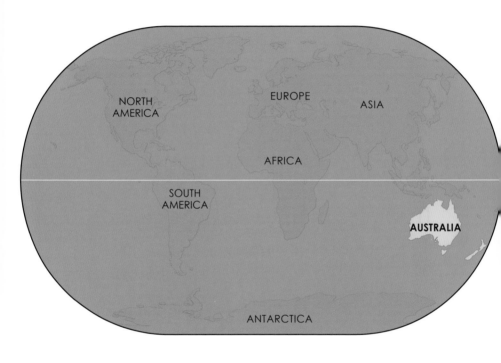

NORTH
AMERICA

EUROPE

ASIA

AFRICA

SOUTH
AMERICA

AUSTRALIA

ANTARCTICA

The largest pieces of land on Earth are continents. There are seven. Australia is the **yellow** continent on this map.

Sydney, Australia

People of Australia

Most people in Australia live in big cities. Some ride a monorail to get from place to place.

A sheep ranch in Australia

Some people in Australia live in the country on farms and ranches.

Aboriginal children learn special dances
from the grown-ups.

Australia's first people are called Aborigines. They have many traditions from long ago.

14

A mother kangaroo carries her baby in a pouch.

Amazing Animals

Australia has unusual animals. Kangaroos hop very fast to go from place to place.

The word koala means "no drink."
Koalas get most of their water from their food.

Koalas live in trees. They eat the leaves. They sleep most of the time.

The outback in Australia

Land and Water

The center of Australia is dry and is called the outback. The outback is hot during the day and cold at night.

Uluru rock

Uluru rock is in the outback. It is the world's largest rock!

Eucalyptus trees grow in Australia.

Australia has forests with tall trees and many plants. Some are found nowhere else in the world.

24 Beautiful coral and many kinds of fish live in the Great Barrier Reef.

Australia is home to the Great Barrier Reef. It is the world's biggest coral reef.

The Barron Falls in Australia

Rain falls in Australia's low mountains. It creates waterfalls. Then the water flows to the oceans that surround this tiny continent.

Modern Marvels

- The Sydney Opera House is Australia's most famous building.

- Its roof is made of curved shapes.

- Each roof section weighs up to 15 tons. That's as big as two male elephants!

Try It!

How many curved shapes do you see? If you made an unusual building, what would it look like?

Meet a Platypus

- Platypuses live in lakes, swamps, and rivers in Australia.

- They have a bill like a duck.

- They have webbed feet.

- Platypuses are mammals, but they lay eggs.

30

Words You Know

kangaroos

koala

outback

waterfall

Index

Facts for Now

Visit this Scholastic Web site for more information on Australia:
www.factsfornow.scholastic.com
Enter the keyword **Australia**

About the Author

Rebecca Hirsch is a scientist-turned-writer and the
author of many books for young readers.